Love Notes to My Body

OTHER BOOKS BY NICOLE C. AYERS

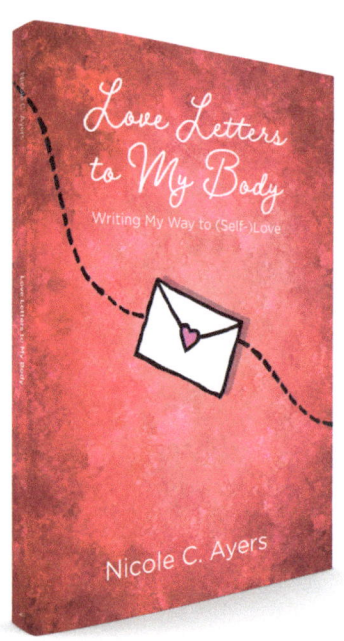

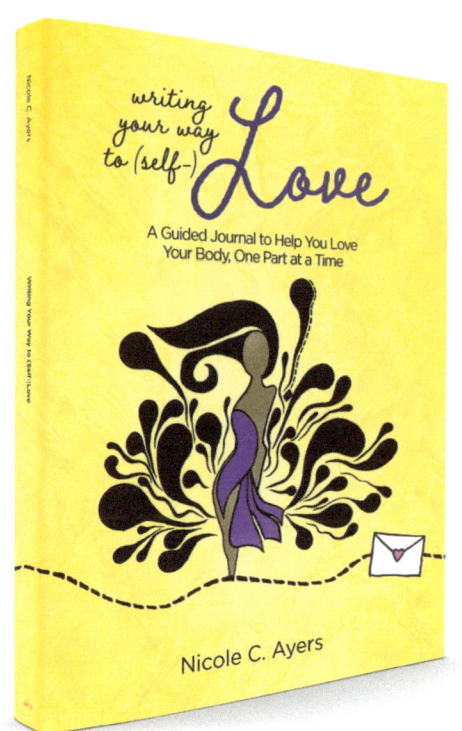

Love Letters to My Body:
Writing My Way to (Self-)Love

Writing My Way to (Self-)Love:
A Guided Journal to Help You
Love Your Body, One Part at a Time

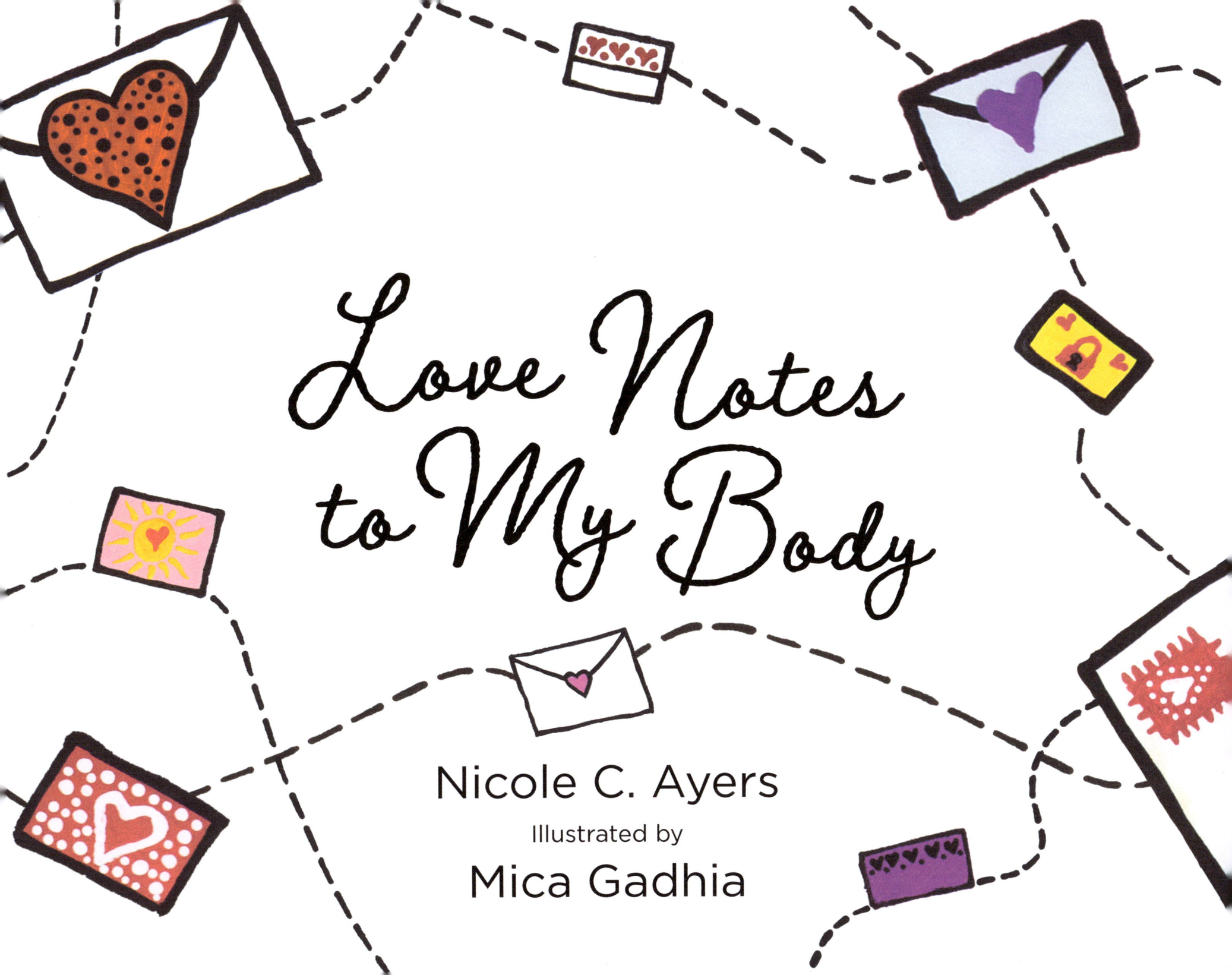

Love Notes to My Body

©2020 by Nicole C. Ayers. All rights reserved. No part of this book may be used or reproduced in any manner whatsoever without written permission from the author, except in the case of brief quotations in critical articles and reviews. For permissions requests, please contact the author at nicole@nicolecayers.com.

Illustrations by Mica Gadhia

Book designed, produced, and published by SPARK Publications
SPARKpublications.com
Charlotte, North Carolina

Printed in the United States of America.
Softcover, February 2020, ISBN: 978-1-943070-81-7
E-book, February 2020, ISBN: 978-1-943070-82-4
Library of Congress Control Number: 2020900972

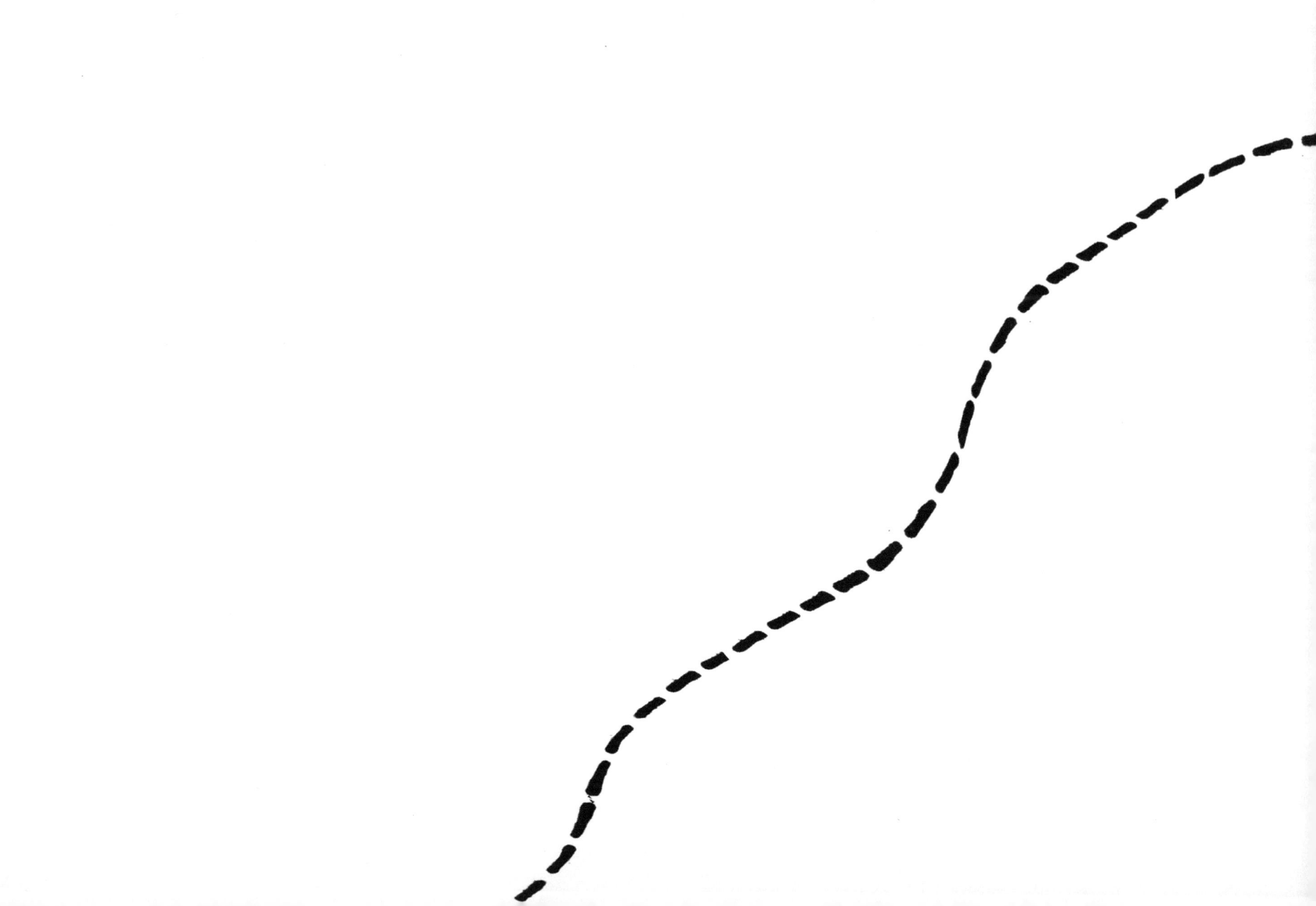

Dedication

I dedicate this book to my body.

You've carried me a long way.

Thank you. I love you. All of you.

~Nicole C. Ayers

I dedicate this book to my younger self . . .

we've come so far.

~Mica Gadhia

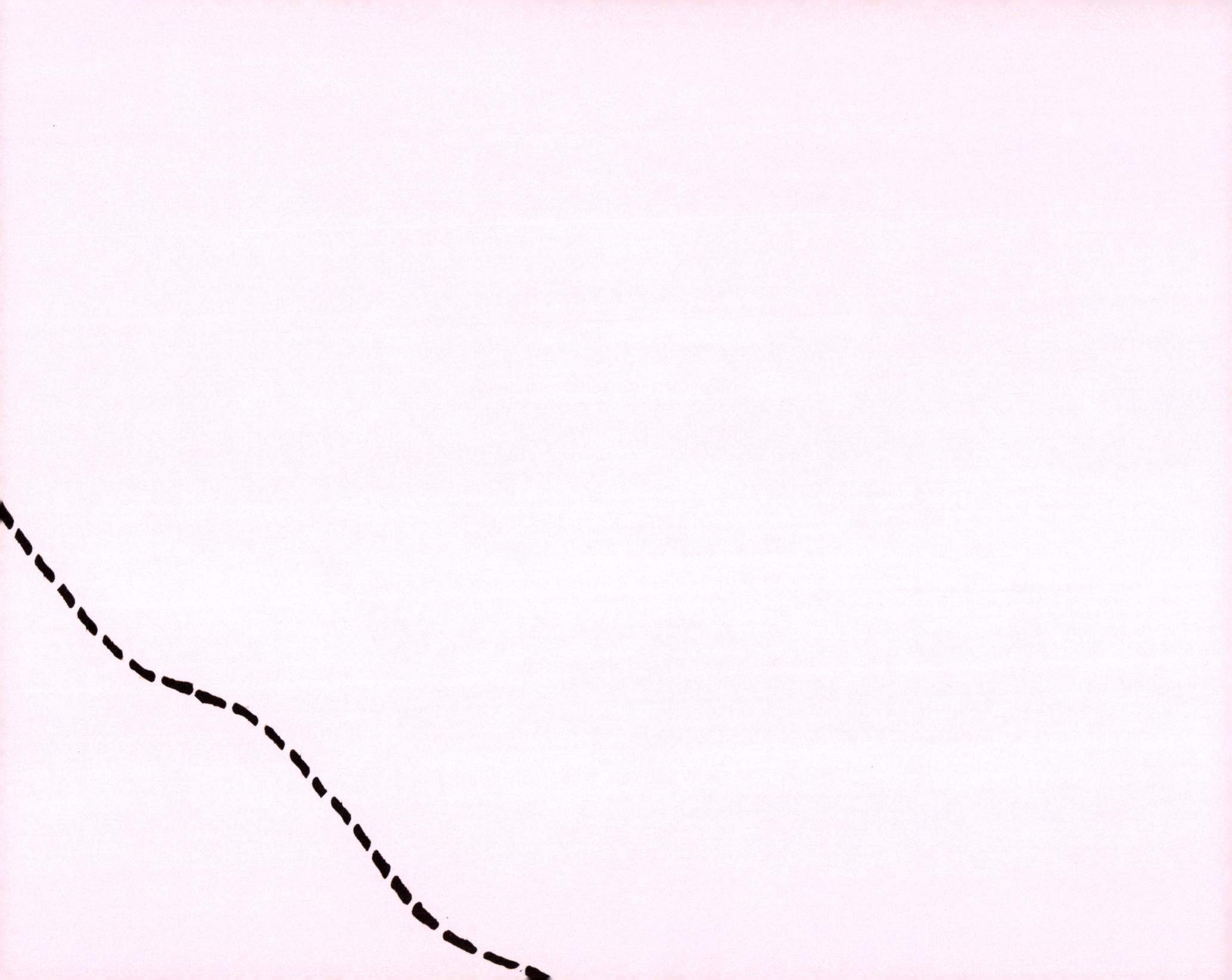

Dear Nicole,

Do you love me?

____Yes ____No ____Maybe ____Sometimes ____Never

Love, Your Body

Love Notes to My Body

SECTION 1

My Body's Parts

Dear Hair,

Thank you for crowning my head with your lustrous shine. You are so flexible—I can wear so many styles—and healthy. Your bold color brings me joy every time I glimpse a rainbow-infused strand. Most of all, I love the freedom you represent, freedom to be independent, to be creative, to be playful, to be noticed, to be my true self.

Love, Me

Dear Eyebrows,

I love your wildness. I'm sorry for the years of torture I made you endure—hot wax and wicked thread—all in an attempt to tame you, to make you shapely, to make you into something somebody else decided you should be.

Now, it makes me chuckle to see you grow however you please. And that strand of white is just right. Thank you for showing me that loving myself, loving my body, loving you, doesn't mean conforming to anybody else's painful beauty expectations.

Love, Me

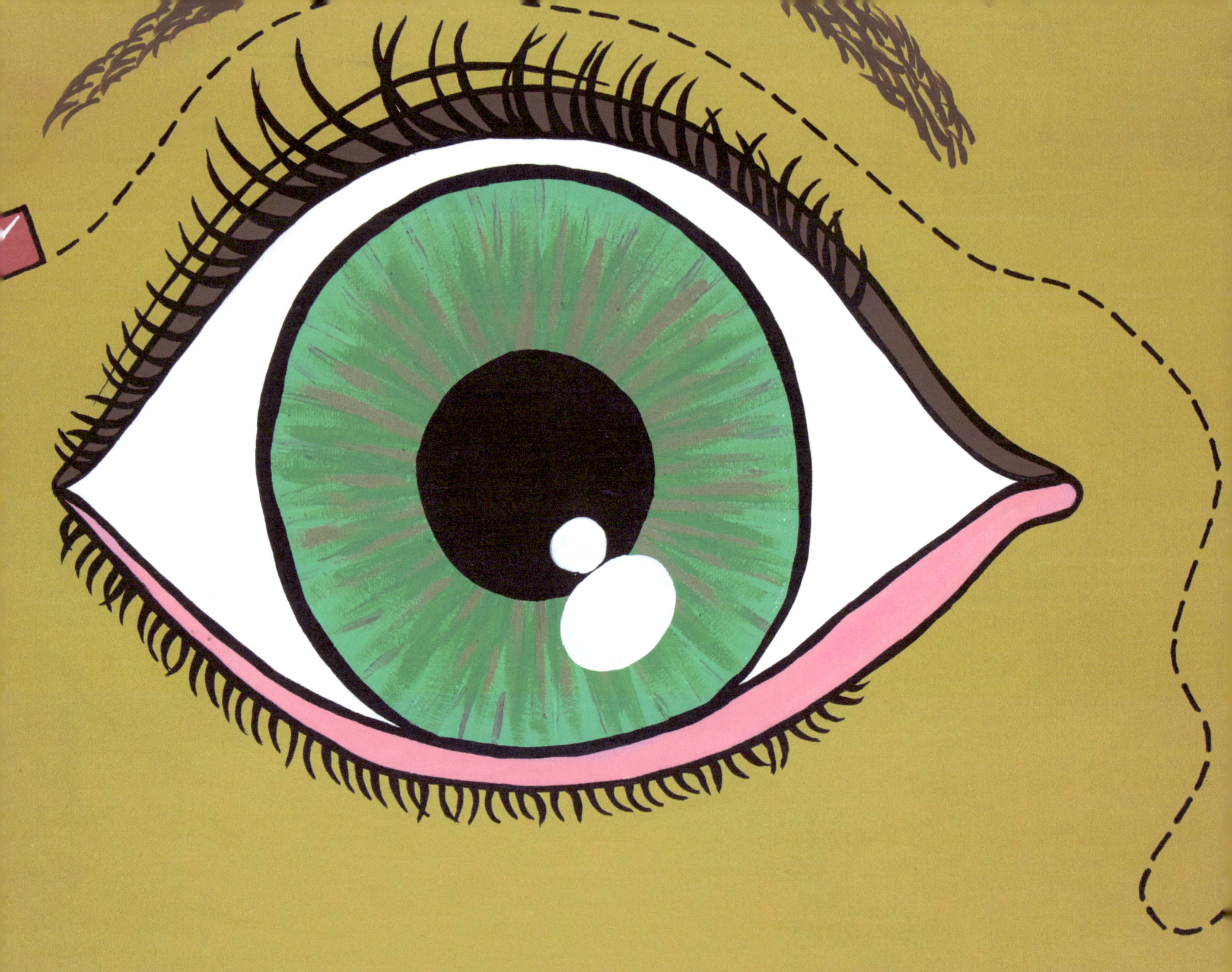

Dear Eyes,

Hazel green flecked with gold, fringed in dark lashes, you are so beautiful. I thank you for seeing the world's wonders—from Alaskan glaciers to my daughters' faces. For the countless words you've read for pleasure, for learning, for editing client manuscripts with Ayers Edits. For the colors that swirl around me, decorating my life with a richness I revel in.

Love, Me

Dear Ears,

Thank you for your willingness to listen. It's a joy to hear my husband, Terry, whisper, "I love you," to know a heart-to-heart is coming when a little-girl voice lobs a heavy question from the backseat of the car, to immerse myself in *Nicole's Love Grooves* when I'm writing. Thank you, too, for carrying the weight of the adornments I use to show a little piece of myself to the world.

Love, Me

Dear Nose,

I have always liked you, especially your shape. You're just right for my face. And I appreciate how sensitive you are. You alert me so I can avoid gross shenanigans and revel in delicious scents. Your guidance is so appreciated.

Love, Me

Dear Cheeks,

I think you are so darn cute. But my love affair with you didn't really begin until I saw you on my child's face.

When I was a kid, people always commented on your chubbiness. And you know the word "chubby" gave me pause. It made me wonder if I was chubby and what I needed to do to not be described as fat because I received so many messages that being fat was bad.

And then I had a baby who looks a lot like me. And she has gorgeous cheeks. They are so round and sweet and cold when I smooch them. And I realized that you, *my* Cheeks, are round and sweet. I don't know if you're cold when smooched as I can't smooch you myself. I love the way my face looks, the softness that comes with you, sweet Cheeks.

Your roundness when I smile helps me imbue kindness to the world, and I sure do like that.

Love, Me

Dear Lips,

Do you remember winning "Best Lips" in the high school senior superlatives? You are quite kissable. Lipstick is my favorite cosmetic because of your lovely, full shape. But my favorite thing about you is your smile. It brightens my day and helps me connect with strangers.

Love, Me

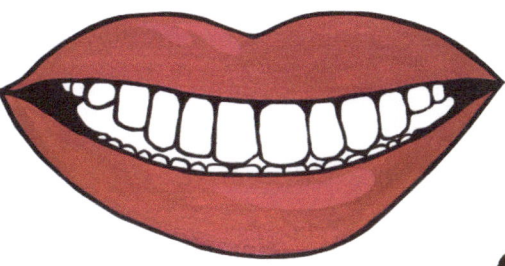

Dear Teeth,

Thank you for your pearly straightness. And without braces—wow! I'm eternally grateful you've given me a smile to be proud of. I forgive those calcium-deposit spots, the cavities in the molars with deep crevices, and the wisdom-teeth shenanigans. You remind me to embrace all of myself. And I love the tiny chip in one of you that reminds me of my glorious imperfections.

Love, Me

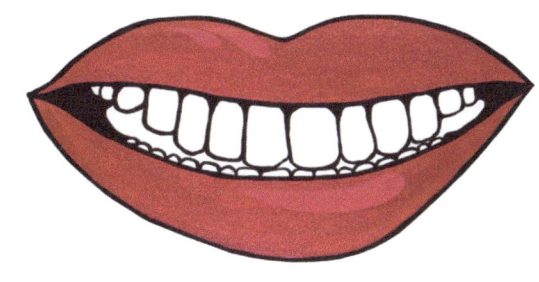

Dear Neck,

Thank you for being the strong base for my brain. You hold my head high, even when I've spent too many hours looking at my computer screen and given you cramps. I promise to love you with slow, sensual rolls and stretches more often.

Love, Me

Dear Collarbones,

Should I call you Clavicles? That sounds very formal. I'll stick with Collarbones. I love the frame you provide Neck and Face, and I think it's so cool that your delicate presence allows my arms to be supported as they hang freely. So often I've looked in the mirror and admired the way you jutted out. You made me feel skinny(er) when I was struggling to love the parts of me with more padding. Sometimes you were the only thing I wasn't criticizing about my body. Thank you for not letting your beloved status make you smug as I learned to love the rest of me.

Love, Me

Dear Shoulders,

When I think of you, it's usually in the metaphorical sense of what load you are carrying. Or how I have always loved the graceful curve of you as you glide from my neck. I've often thought you looked delicate, but really, you have shown that you are strong beyond measure as you've hauled my heavy bag of "should" around for years. Isn't it funny how you can't see the truth of something until you really look at it? Thank you for that perspective.

Love, Me

Dear Arms,

I love you for the hugs you've offered others, for the times you've carried too many bags just so I could make only one trip from the car to the house, for the support you've given in yoga poses. I love your jiggly biceps and your muscular triceps. I love all of you.

Love, Me

Dear Hands,

Hi there, hands. You have held so many things dear to me: countless books, colorful pens, Terry's hands, my babies. Your strength and capacity to hold what comes makes me feel strong. And capable.

I'm having fun using you to balance as I work on getting upside down in handstands. Checking this off my bucket list has reminded me of the power we hold.

There's this little nodule in my left palm that is giving me pause. I wonder what you're trying to tell me. Are you okay? Know we're in this together, no matter what. I love you.

Love, Me

Dear Fingers,

I love how your touch provides me with a connection to myself, with my loved ones, with my pets, with the world at large. I learn so much thanks to your curiosity and exploration. You're an intrepid leader in helping me discern what is going on around me.

Love, Me

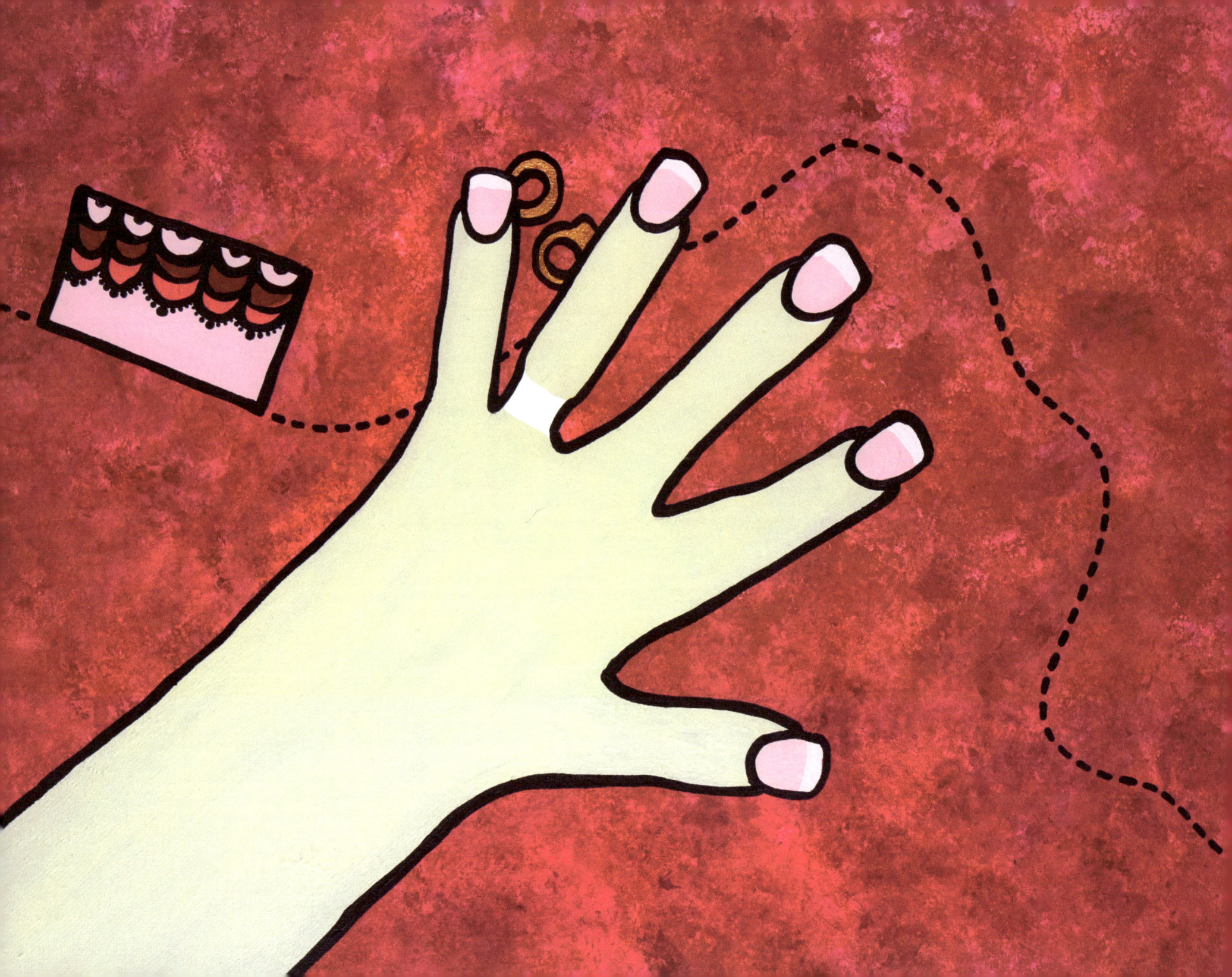

Dear Ring Finger on My Left Hand,

Thank you for supporting my marriage day after day, year after year. You have never balked at wearing my wedding rings, even though they've changed your shape and color to a svelte curve and a luminous glow. You wear the symbols of my marriage with pride and love, and you remind me of the commitment I make to my husband, Terry, every day.

Love, Me

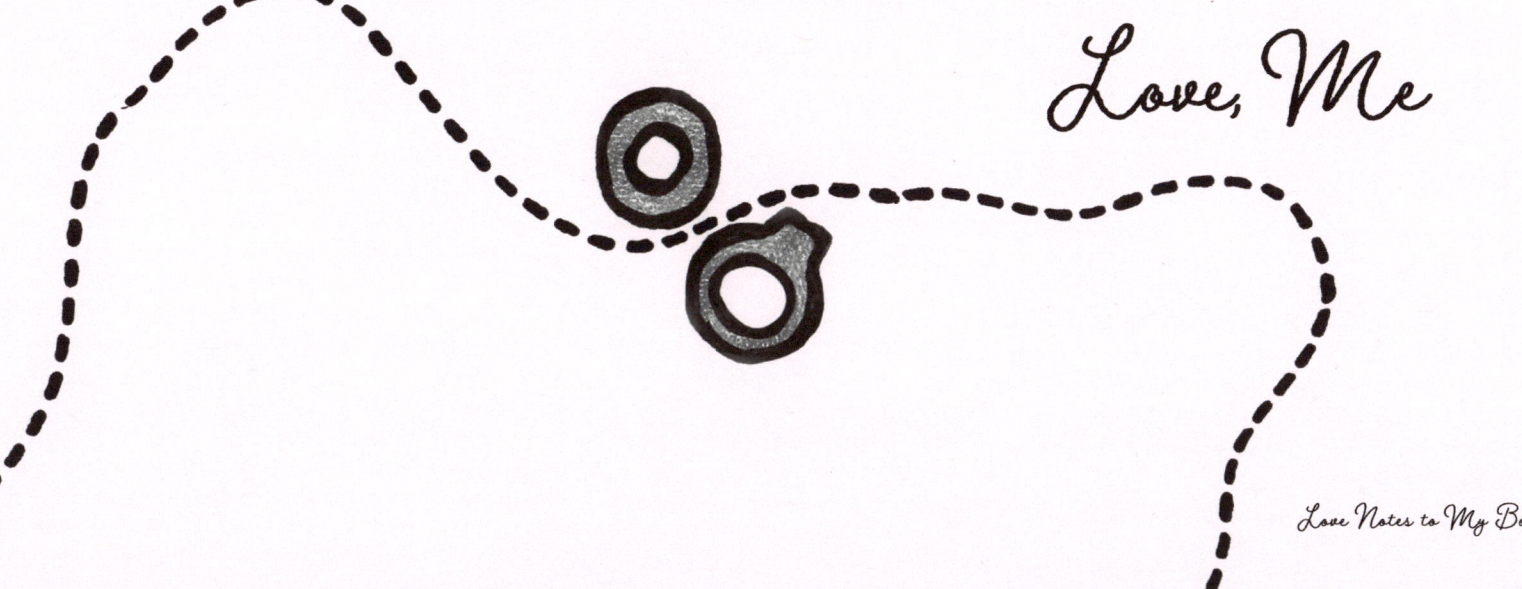

Dear Back,

As the part of me that represents my past, you're a treasure trove of wisdom I can pull from. Thank you for your integrity to stand tall and teach me what I need to know about taking good care of myself. I love your strength, which carries me forward, leaving behind what I no longer need.

Love, Me

Dear Boobs,

After years of judging you as too much or not enough, I want you to know that I think you're perfect. The very fact that you fed tiny humans is a miracle. Your shape, your size, your cleavage (whoa, mama!), and your perkiness (or lack thereof) are all just exactly right for my body.

Love, Me

Dear Belly,

Sweet, jiggly Belly, you make me giggle when I shake you. I treasure the way you stretched to make room for my babies. You are a cozy place to cuddle with your rounded curves, and your strong core keeps me balanced. I love the paradox of your soft strength.

Love, Me

Dear Curves,

You are so sexy! I love the way my hands flow over you in sinuous waves. The landscape is interesting to travel and explore. You create the perfect shape to snuggle my husband, my lover. The soft lines remind me of the perfection and completeness that circles represent. You make me perfect and complete.

Love, Me

Dear Hips,

A wise woman once said the hips don't lie. I agree that you're a truth teller. I remember the first time a yoga teacher said that we store emotions in our hips. I thought that was a bunch of hooey. It only took one long hold in a frog pose to change my mind. I think of your wide, curvy expansiveness, and I think of my deep, intense feelings, and your shape makes perfect sense.

Love, Me

Dear Butt,

I love your out-thereness, your unabashed curves, the way you make my body feel very feminine. Plus, you offer a cozy space to sit when I'm tired. I especially appreciate the padding you provide so that I can sit comfortably in my front-porch chairs.

Love, Me

Dear Vagina,

I feel shy because others will read this love note and know that I think you're amazing. Also because I'm a bit of a prude. Well, maybe not a prude, but definitely private.

I still love you, though, Vagina. You've given me great pleasure and intimate connections. You've also healed from trauma and unwanted attention. Standing up for you has allowed me to find my voice in unexpected ways. Your vulnerability and resilience are admirable.

Love, Me

Dear Thighs,

Thank you for your strength, your stability. You kept my knee in place for twenty years after I refused much-needed surgery. But you didn't stop there. Your toughness showed up during every physical-therapy appointment. Your beautiful, long muscles said, "Rely on me as you learn to walk again. I will carry you." That breaks my heart open in the best way. Thank you.

Love, Me

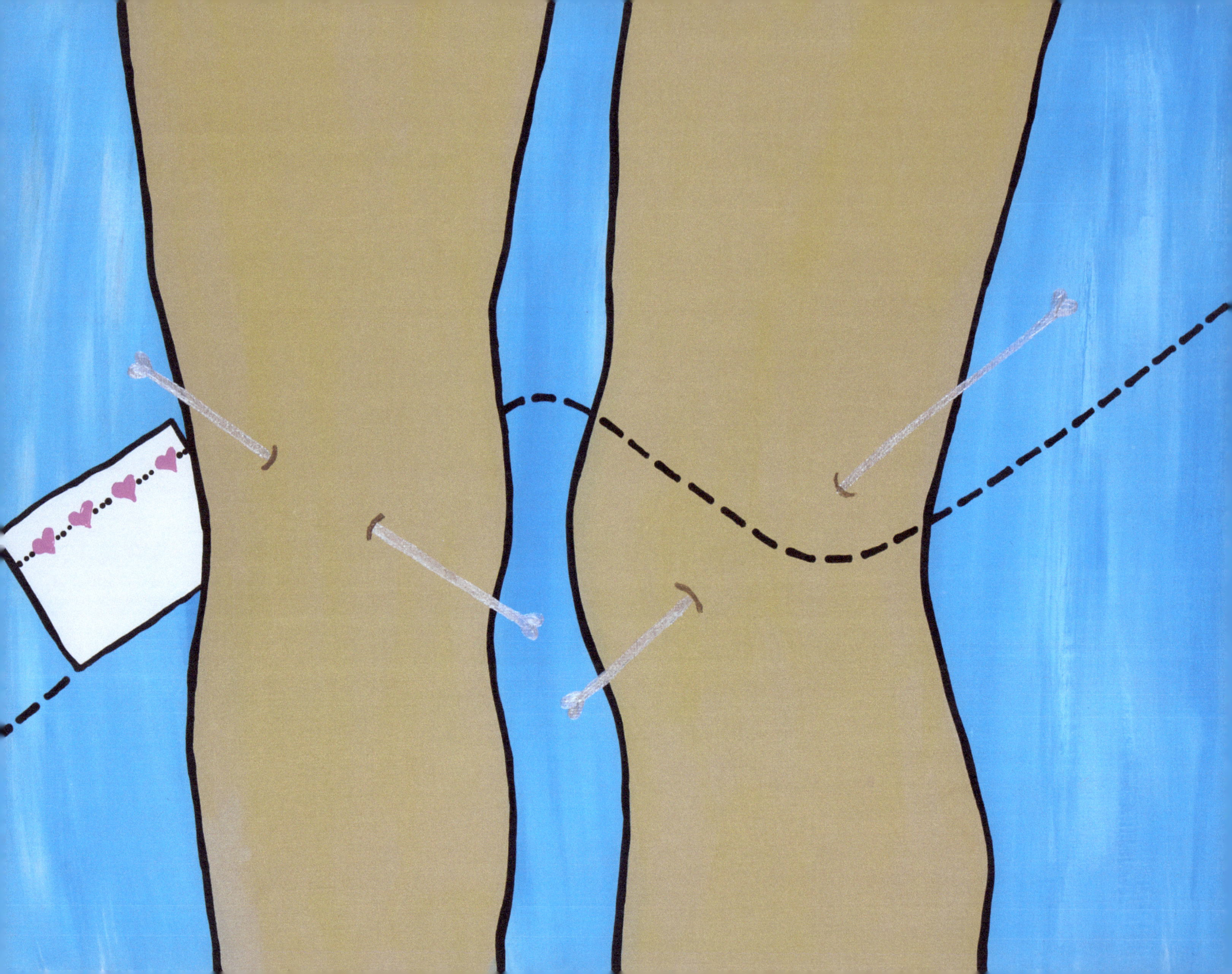

Dear Knees,

Thank you for bending and straightening, bending and straightening, bending and straightening—with ease and through pain. Thank you for the many times you've healed and for welcoming extra hardware to keep me in motion.

You ache because you were wounded. You tried so hard to keep me upright. But I still fell. And I'm okay. Sometimes you have to let me fall. You don't have to hold me up by yourself. I love you so much and thank you for your strong support and deep loyalty.

Love, Me

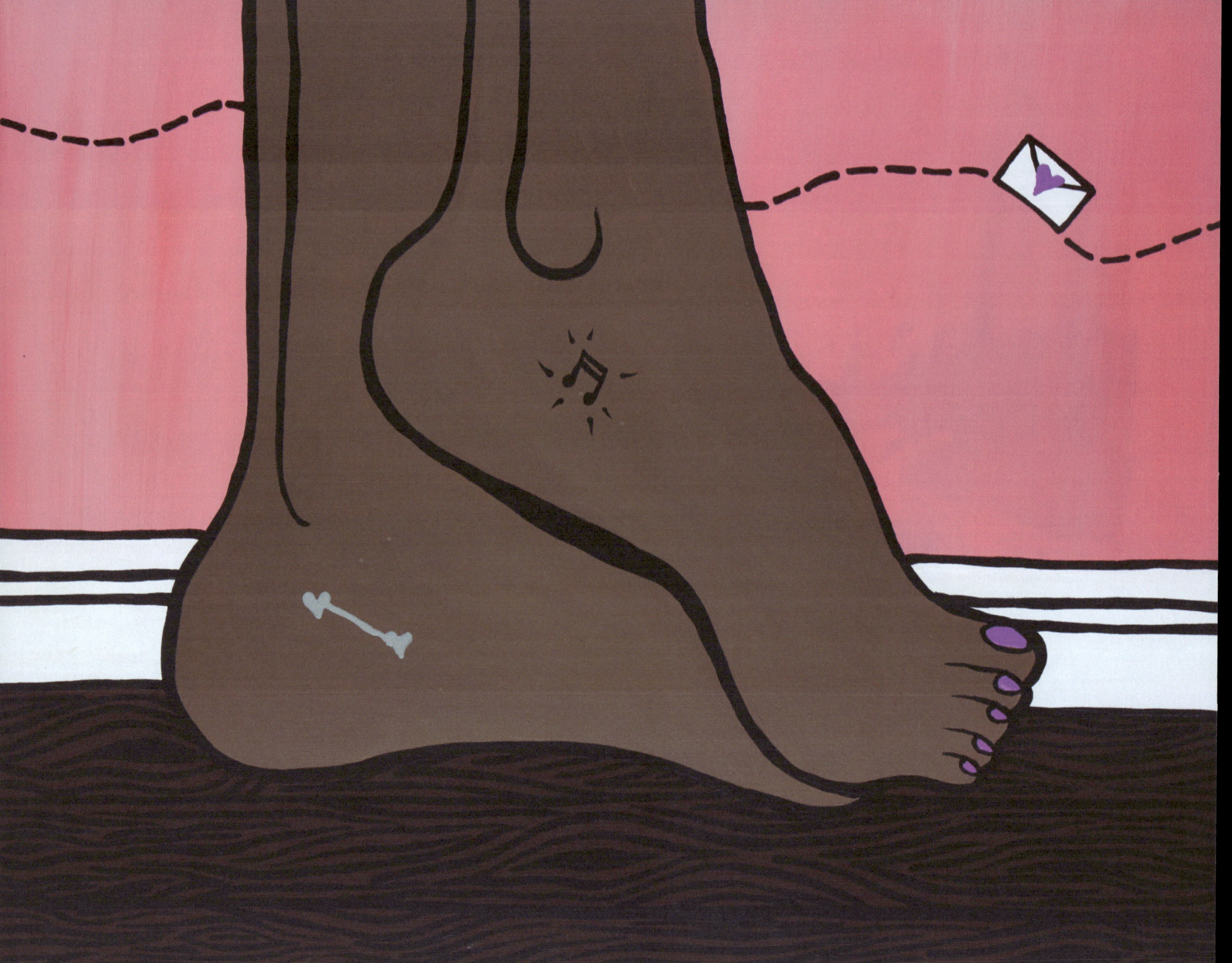

Dear Ankles,

I love the symphony of creaks you make when I circle you round and round in a deep stretch. Rightie, I'm not sure why you're making so much noise. Leftie, you have a good excuse. I think some of my left knee's hardware has migrated down to you. At least, TSA agents seem to think so because they give you a special patdown every single time we fly. Keep singing, ladies!

Love, Me

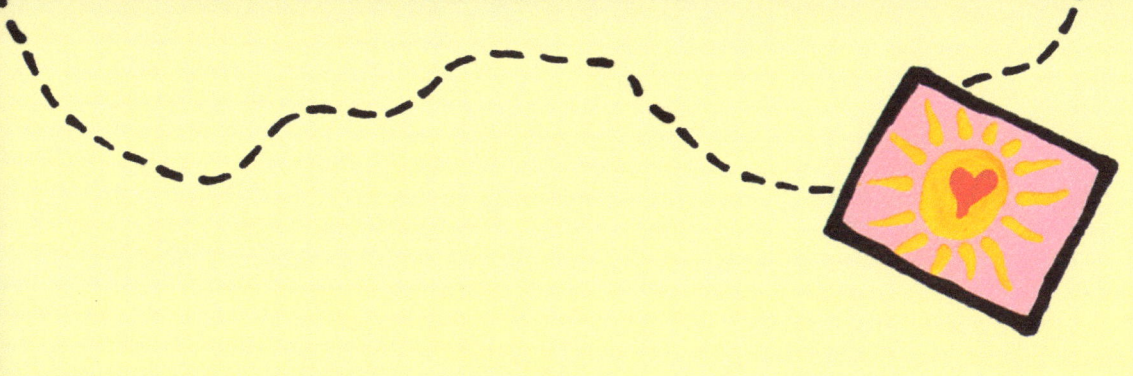
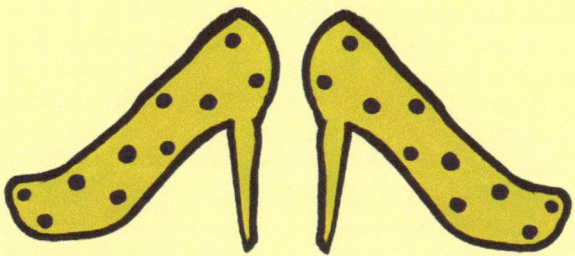

Dear Feet,

Thank you for the many miles you have carried me. For sliding me across dance floors. For grounding me. For bringing me barefoot joy when I stick you in the sand. And I love you even when wet grass makes you squeamish. You're allowed a quirk. In fact, I embrace it.

Love, Me

Dear Pinky Toe,

I am wrapping you in a protective bubble of love. I have accidentally knocked you into things so many times, creating pain and bruises. But you just heal and hang out. Little piggies get a bad rap for running away, but you never have. You are loyal always. Thank you.

Love, Me

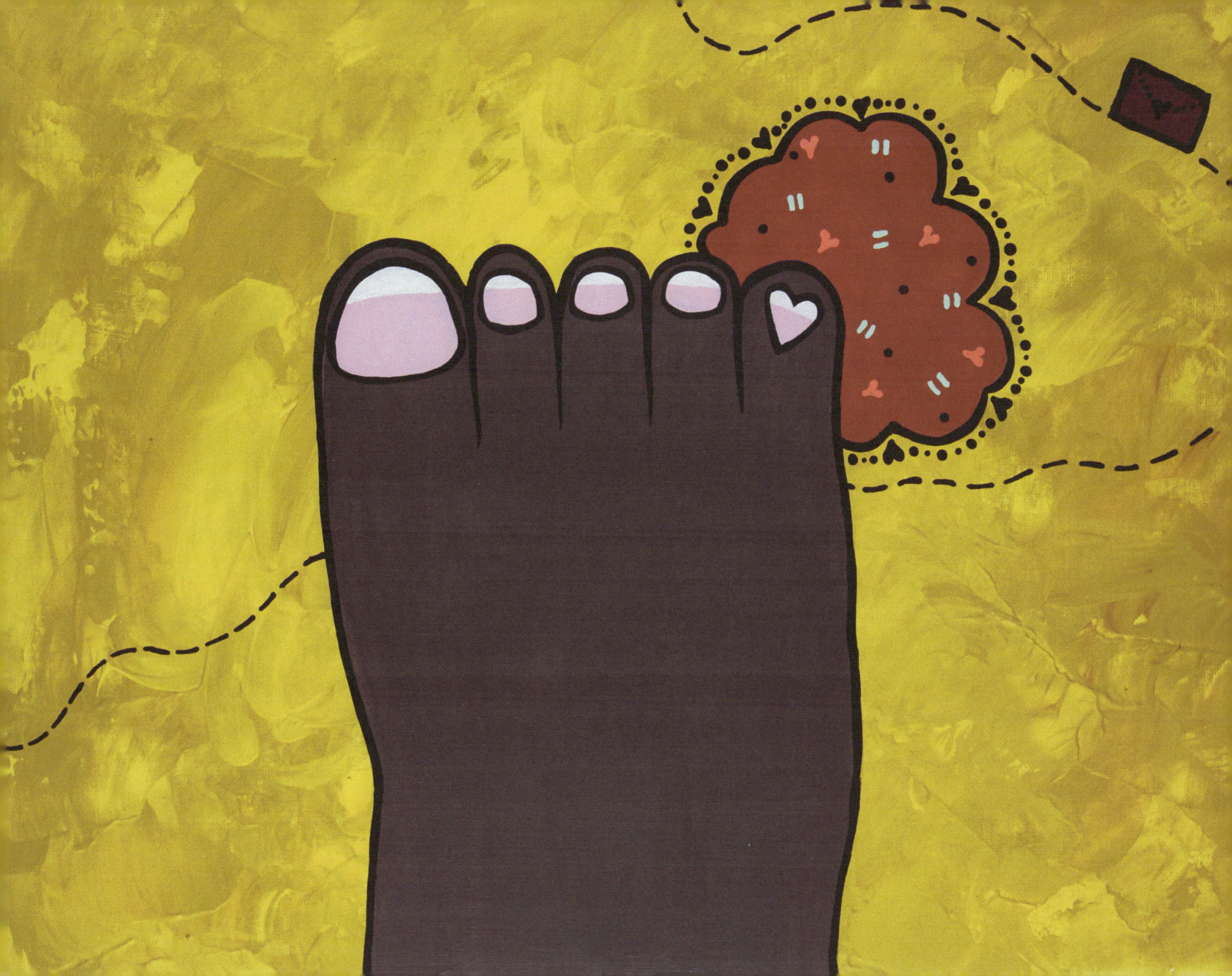

Dear Toenails,

Your colorful shine delights me when I catch you peeking from my shoes. Or when I glance down at my bare feet and see your sparkle. Painting you is a joy as I get to play with color. Thank you for being the canvas that showcases my artwork. You're an easy pick-me-up when I need a boost.

Love, Me

SECTION 2

My Skin and Her Friends

Love Notes to My Body

Dear Skin,

Thank you for the millions of nerve endings that bring me pleasure and comfort, that absorb the sun to make me feel like a lizard, that rub against the cool sheets when I wake. It's so easy to love you when I suds you up or smooth body cream along your softness.

Love, Me

Dear Hair Covering My Entire Body,

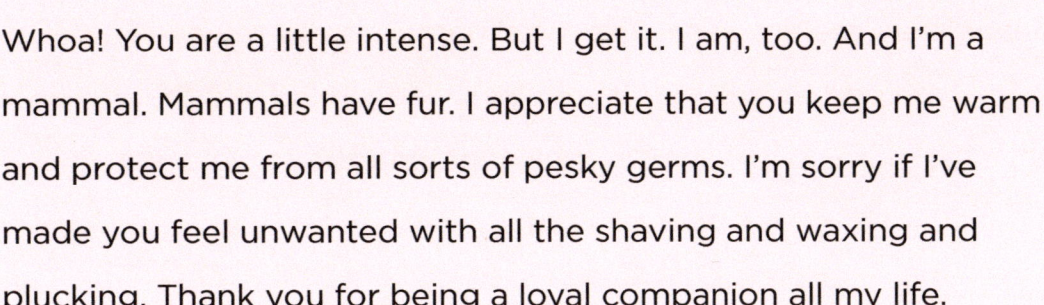

Whoa! You are a little intense. But I get it. I am, too. And I'm a mammal. Mammals have fur. I appreciate that you keep me warm and protect me from all sorts of pesky germs. I'm sorry if I've made you feel unwanted with all the shaving and waxing and plucking. Thank you for being a loyal companion all my life.

Love, Me

Dear Crow's-Feet,

Thank you for reflecting my life's joys to the world. I love the idea that my smiles and laughter create creases that hold happiness by my eyes so I may "see" it. Some people call you laugh lines, and while I like that, too, I like crow's-feet more. Crows are so intelligent, and they love shiny treasure. I like thinking I'm wise enough to find my treasure in joy.

Love, Me

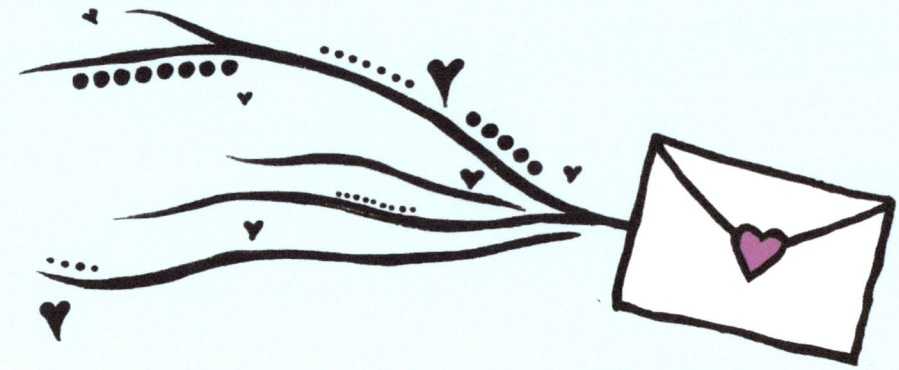

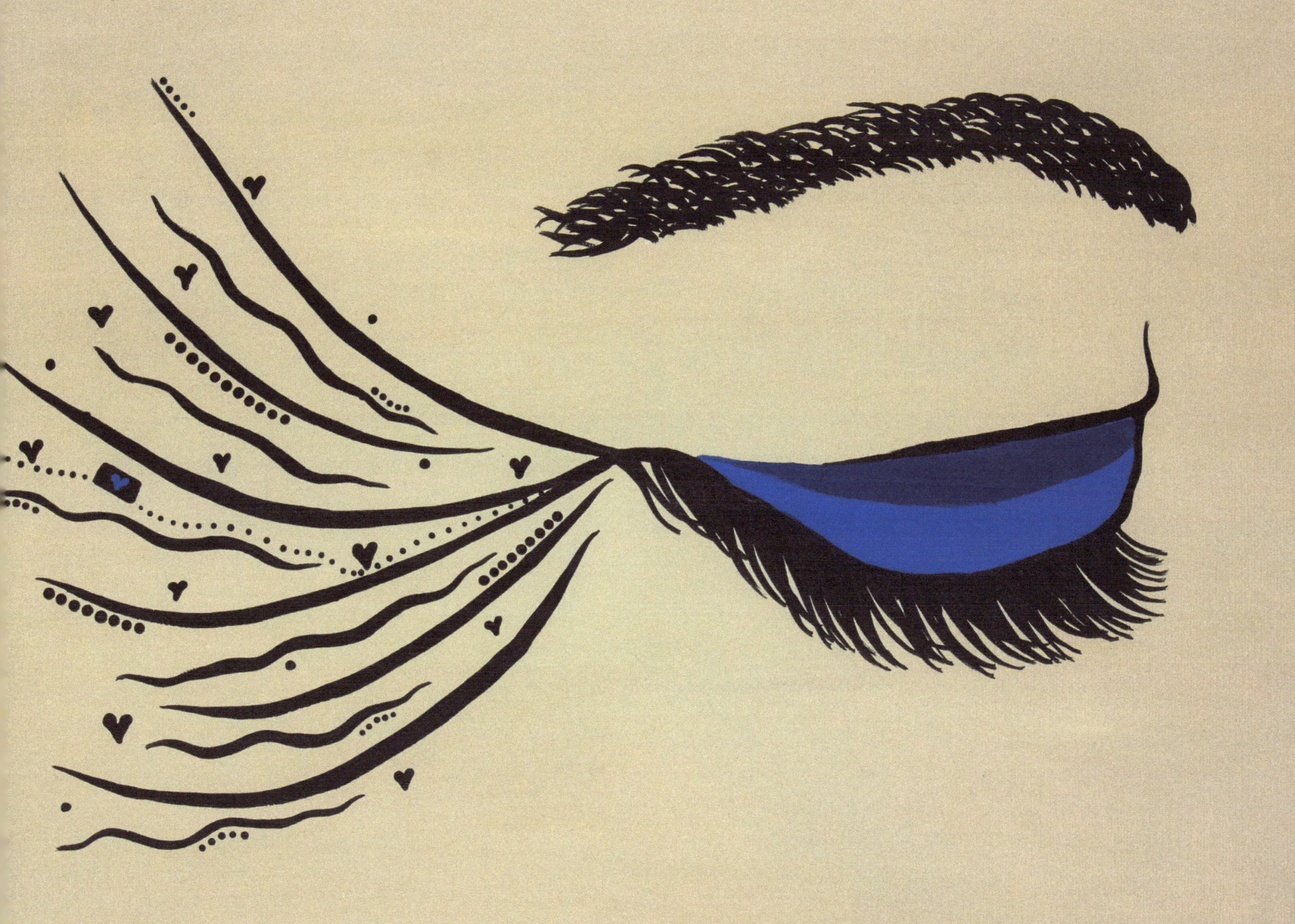

Dear Freckles,

Man, you are cute. I didn't give you much thought most of my life, but now that I see you reflected on my daughters' gorgeous faces, I am so in love with you. You're a reminder of the sun's kisses, little dots of warmth that shine from my face. I am so glad you decided to land here.

Love, Me

Dear White-and-Dark Patch on My Left Ribcage,

You've been such a benign presence all my life that I'm always surprised when someone asks if I'm okay and then points to you. I love your constant presence, which reminds me I'm unique and malleable, open to change. I remember your glossy whiteness when I was a little girl. Then the summer after fifth grade, I wore a bikini for the first time, and basking in the sun browned you forevermore.

The dermatologist told me you have some funky name that I can't remember, but that you weren't harmful to me in any way. I told her I already knew that.

Love, Me

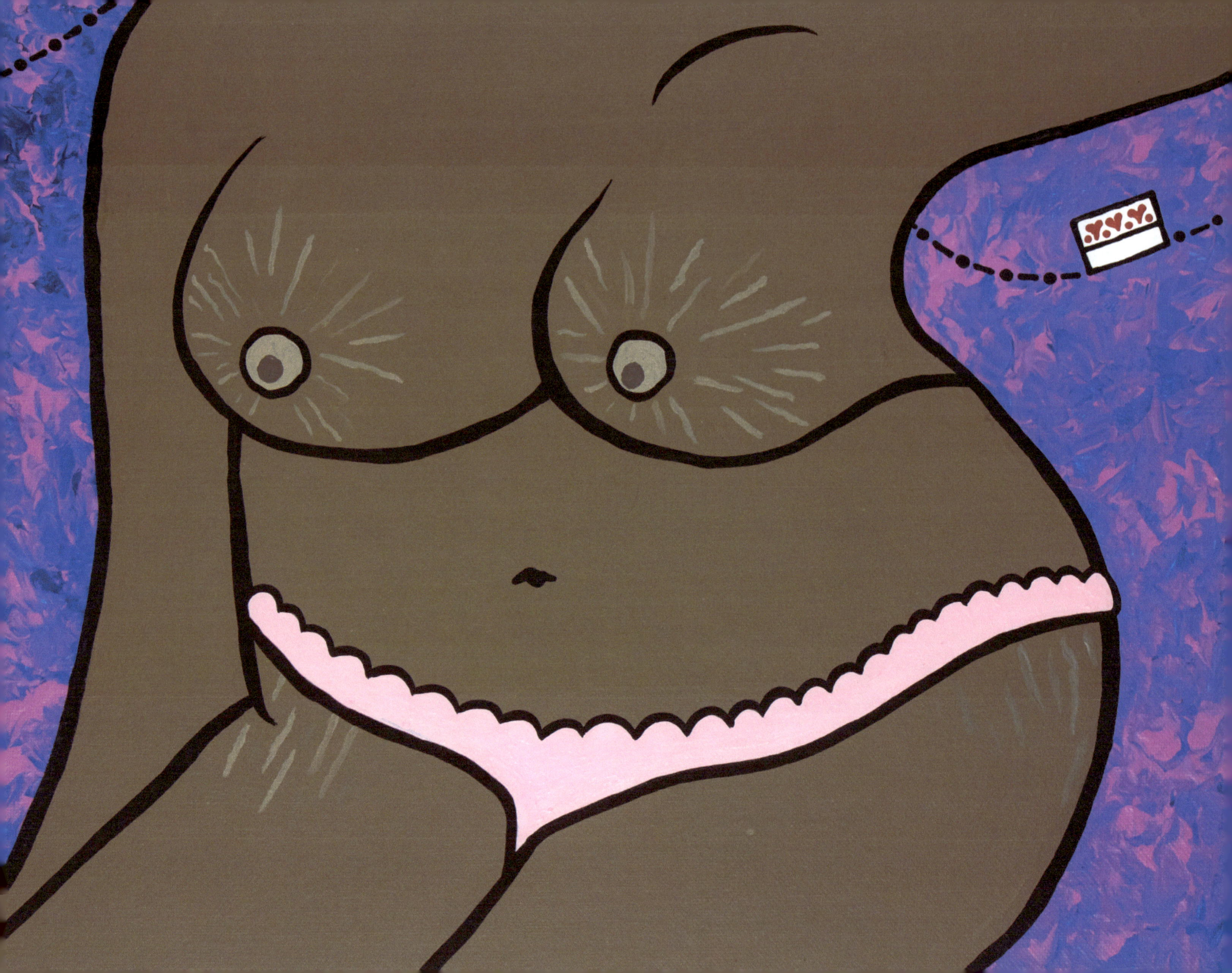

Dear Stretch Marks,

You remind me of when my body burst into womanhood. You see, you aren't the stretch marks women get on their abdomens when they're having babies. Nope, you guys exist on my breasts and my hips.

One day I had a little girl's body, and the next I was walking around with a woman's shape. It's as if my true form was called forth and my body responded, "Yes, yes, here I am. Watch me bloom!" At first I was confused about what to do with my newfound roundness and how to handle the responses—solicited and unsolicited—I received, but now I'm so grateful for my curvy shape. Thank you for reminding me that my body was so excited to be in its true form.

Love, Me

Dear Rough Patches on My Heels,

I see you there, your yellowing thick skin, the cracks running along the callouses. Welcome. I know it's trendy to have baby-smooth feet, but here's the thing—I'm not a baby. I want to celebrate the wisdom I've acquired. I've walked a lot of miles on these feet, some of them bare, and I've earned your protection.

I want to take good care of you, not so you'll leave, but so you'll know you're loved. I'll soften you with moisturizer; I'll exfoliate you on sandy beach walks and with decadent sugar scrubs that feel like a little present for you.

Love, Me

Dear Scars,

Quite a few of you have taken up residence on and in me. Those of you on my knees get the most attention. Then there's you, my C-section Scar, which I don't even see very often as you're usually covered with hair. I feel you sometimes, though, and I'm always grateful when I think about what you represent. Then there are those of you that no one knows about, like the tiny one at the top of my left ear from the time I pierced it at the beach, and the one on my cervix from when I was pregnant and had a cerclage to avoid preterm labor. And of course, there are those of you who are present on my soul—your presence means a lot to me because you show that I've healed those heartbreaks.

I love you all. Your puckered beauty shows everything I've survived.

Love, Me

SECTION 3

My Internal Lovelies

Dear Skeleton,

I want to break into a rollicking rendition of "Dem Bones" to celebrate you, and if I'm singing, I gotta dance, right? All thanks to you. I love how you're a body within my body, the framework upon which my muscles balance.

You connect in magical ways to allow me to move in supple, graceful resilience. I'm most impressed with the way you knit yourself back together when you were broken. You didn't let a fracture keep you from rejoining. That's the ultimate lesson in forgiveness. And while there may always be a fissure to show you were injured, it also shows you were healed.

Love, Me

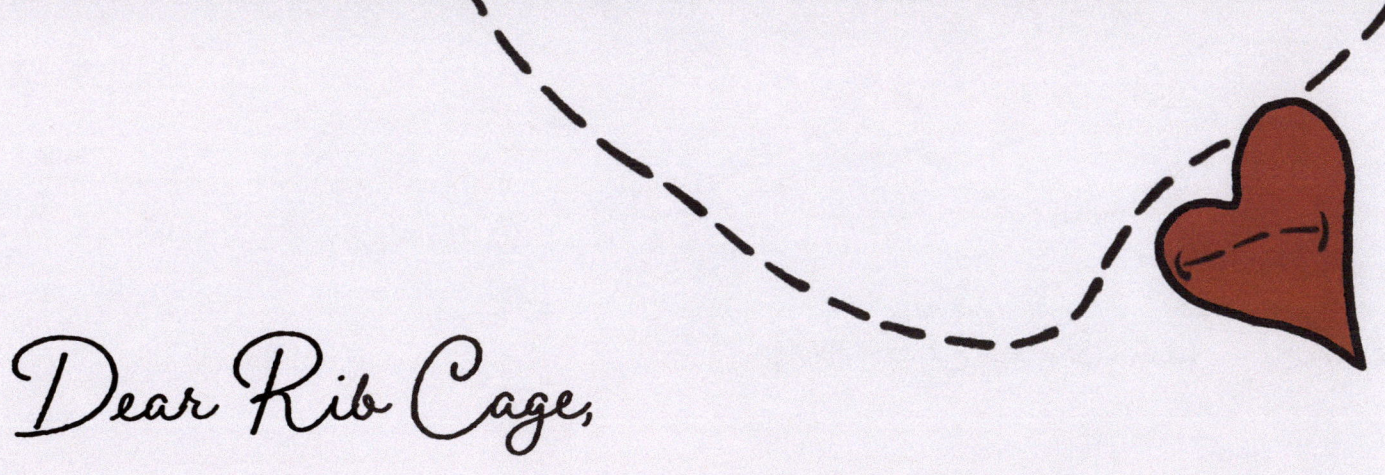

Dear Rib Cage,

I love to think of you as this badass xylophone that plays a mean rhythm to protect my heart and lungs. You look a bit fragile, thin as you are, with empty spaces between. But I wonder if it's those spaces that allow you to expand and be strong when you need to be.

I broke one of you the last time I went skydiving. And last winter, I broke another of you coughing. Yet despite your fragility, you protect me, hold my heart space open, create room for me to breathe.

Love, Me

Dear Cadaver Bone,

I want to share my immense gratitude with you and to the generous soul you grew inside of. I wonder who this person was, if they were a good dancer, what brought them joy.

When I crushed my tibial plateau in a car accident, you stepped in so I didn't have to suffer through a painful bone graft. Your presence allowed my body to heal and replace the bone that had been pulverized.

You've inspired me to be a donor cadaver one day. I can't think of a better way to dispose of my earthly remains than to give everything I can to people who will have a better use for them than I will.

Love, Me

Dear Muscles,

You are an amazing bit of engineering, moving me through life. Let me just say what a marvel you are. I appreciate that sometimes you're so bunched and tight because I'm clinging hard to something, or I've overworked you and neglected your stretching, and you keep performing for me anyway. I don't want you to hurt, so I'm going to treat you to massages and juicy movement practices that show my love and gratitude.

Love, Me

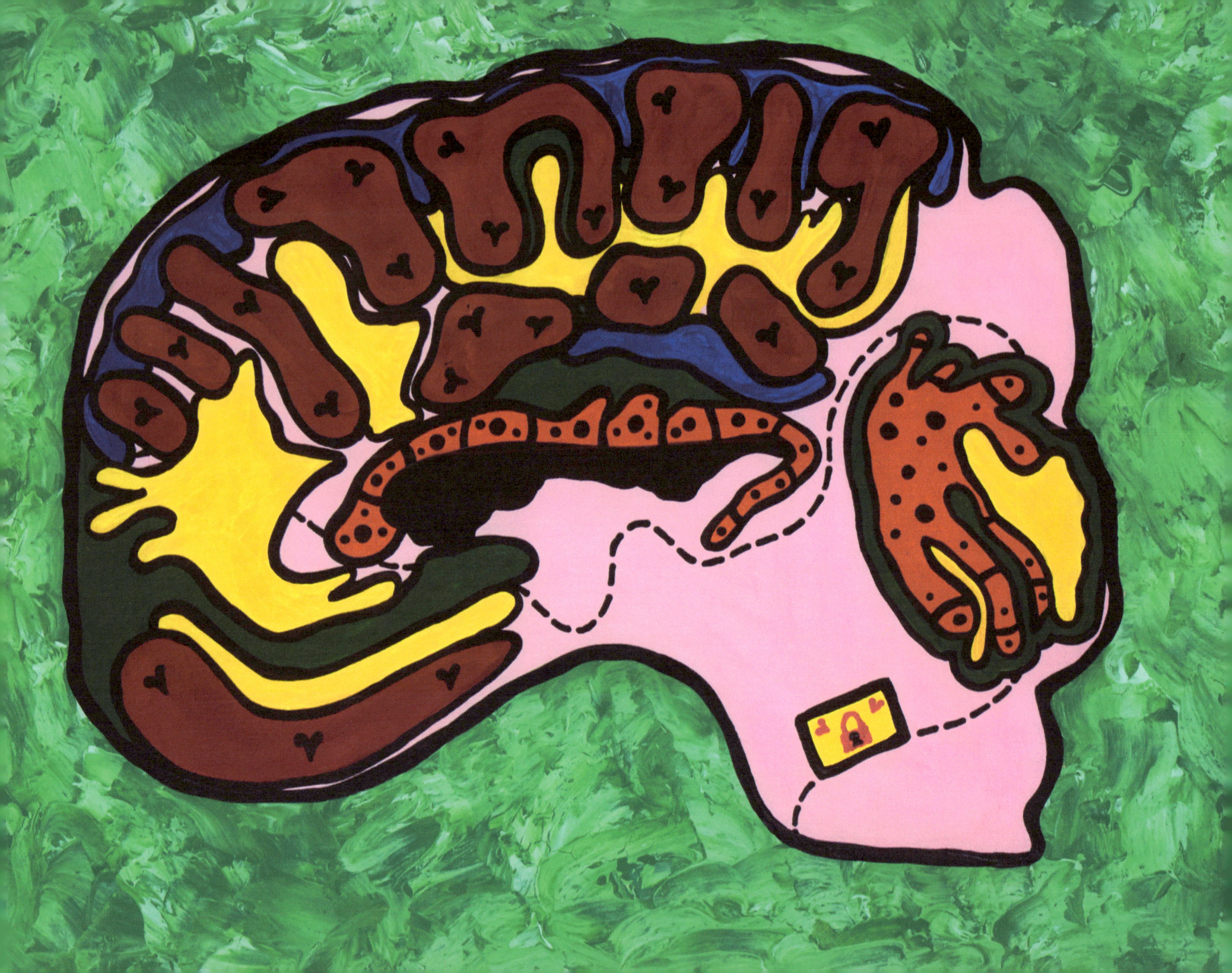

Dear Brain,

I spend so much time with you, and I never tell you just how amazing you are. As the control system for my body, you are really good at your job. You keep me moving and breathing and thinking and responding, and quite frankly, you don't get enough credit. Your capacity to manage so many different systems to keep me healthy and whole is fantastic. Thank you for taking such good care of me. Your focus is on me and my survival, and I really appreciate that.

I wonder what secrets you hold, what depths you contain, that I have yet to unlock. You're mysterious in the best kind of way—I want to know more.

Love, Me

Dear Taste Buds,

You make everything so yummy! Your super receptors enable me to enjoy delicious meals, savory flavors, sour refreshments, salty fare, spicy tidbits, and sweet desires. Thank you for the zest you bring to my life.

Love, Me

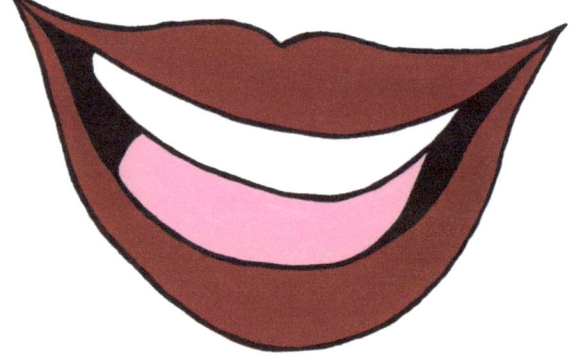

Dear Thyroid,

To say you gave me quite a scare is like saying I may have squeaked a swear word the night I stepped on a palmetto bug with my bare foot.

Turns out, you have lots of nodules, but all are benign. Thank God! So far, none of them have decided to make my life hinky, for which I am also grateful. You lovingly provide support to so many of my systems, and I don't want you to struggle. I love you. And now that I know more about my body, I wonder what truths I wasn't speaking. What words and resentments was I holding inside? I'm paying attention now. I'm here for you.

Love, Me

Dear Heart,

I love you. I thank you. For your timeless consistency. For your compassion. For your empathy. For you perseverance. For your love. For your softness. For your resilience. You continue to break over tragedy. Don't callus. Even though it hurts. This is how you stay motivated to be a changemaker.

When I try to wrap my head around your awesomeness, I get befuddled. I cannot comprehend a rhythmic muscle that beats, never stopping, just to keep me alive. What a gorgeous show of selfless love. How could I not love you in return?

You help me live wide open, even when I'm scared. And I swear you keep growing. Sometimes I think you'll engulf all of me, and I think that is just fine.

Love, Me

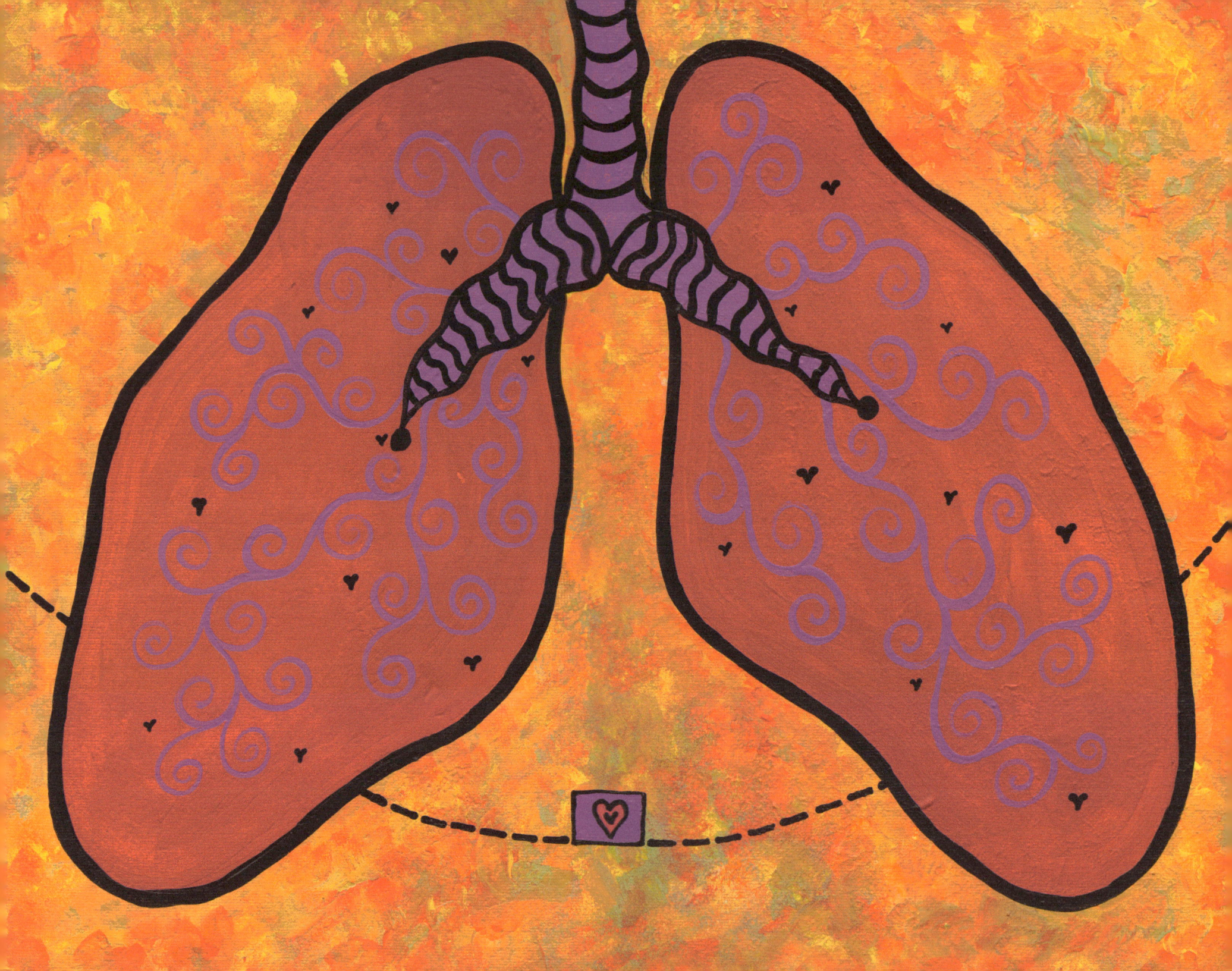

Dear Lungs,

Taking slow, long, deep breaths is such a pleasure. I love to feel you inflating with oxygen and then slowly releasing carbon dioxide. The act of deep breathing calms me so much, and I'm grateful for the role you play in bringing me peace.

I also want to tell you how sorry I am that I filled you with cigarette smoke for years. I know I hurt you. Please forgive me. And thank you for healing yourself from the wounds I inflicted. What a beautiful reminder you are that I can heal what has been hurt when I remove toxicity from my life.

Love, Me

Dear Liver and Kidneys and Other Detoxifying Organs,

I had no idea just how hard you've been working to keep my body clean, especially when I've abused you with craft beer, salty fries, and chocolate-covered, cream-filled doughnuts. You've been quietly doing your job without any expectation of praise. Thank you for your loving care.

Love, Me

Dear Uterus,

Thanks seem inadequate. You carried my two precious daughters and let them safely grow. You did your job beautifully, and I am so, so grateful. May you live in comfortable retirement the rest of our days, knowing that you served me well.

Love, Me

SECTION 4

My Body's Creations

Dear Blood,

Ruby red, thick, and viscous—you're the sustaining river of my life. I love the swiftness with which you carry cells around my body to fight disease, oxygen to nourish my organs, nutrients to feed my energy needs, and waste to relieve me of toxins. Thank you for making more of yourself so I can share your O+ vitality with people who need it. You have my sincere appreciation and awe for the ingenious way you congeal, harden, and scab when I've been injured.

Love, Me

Dear Tears,

You live so close to the surface most days and provide me with a release that is so cleansing. When my heart is bursting with love, your prickling allows me to release the overflow of emotion in my heart. You help me connect to my people, strangers, and sometimes fictional souls with empathy and affection. And when I feel broken, or the world's tragedies are too heavy, you help me release my grief and let it go. You are beloved.

Love, Me

Dear Poop,

Thank you for letting go. For years, I wasted time trying to control you. But now I know the pleasure of a great poo on my own personal throne, complete with a bidet, and I will never go back to those constipated days again. Many thanks for showing me how good releasing what needs to go (#2) can be.

Love, Me

Dear Period,

I thought when we broke up that I'd never want to see your bloodred stains again. I definitely didn't want your heavy flow or your flu-like miasma to settle over me. And let's be honest, you overstayed your welcome a number of times, arriving unexpectedly and lasting weeks on end.

But I miss you. I do. I miss your cyclical cadence, the backbeat you provided, your natural rhythms.

Love, Me

Dear Voice,

Hello, darling! I owe you an apology for all the times I shushed you without thought to your feelings, stuffing you down as if you didn't matter. And I'm sorry for the many times I've said I'd rather dance naked in public than sing in front of people because you sound terrible. That's not really true. I adore listening to you. Belting out anthems in my car makes me so happy.

I'm learning quickly how vulnerable I feel when I use you to speak up for what is true. But also how strong I feel. Thank you for showing me that I can be both vulnerable and strong at the same time. I can be transparent and real, or I can be opaque and fake. You let me choose every time I open my mouth. I'm going to try really hard to choose bravely.

Love, Me

Dear Body,

Do you love me?

_____Yes   _____No   _____Maybe   _____Sometimes   _____Never

Love, Nicole

Acknowledgments

My Deepest Gratitude

To my Divi, for your providence in the creation of this book, in the creation of my life.

To my sisters on this journey, for showing me the ways that you love your bodies. For showing me the ways that you don't.

To my parents, for giving me life, for fusing your chromosomes to create this body of mine, for always doing your best to love and care for me.

To my friends and family, for loving and encouraging me and promising to read this book. You are too many to name individually, but I love each and every one of you.

To the person who donated their body so I could receive their cadaver bone and heal from a terrible accident with less pain. Along with Mary Roach and her book *Stiff*, you've inspired me to donate my body when I die.

To my teachers, whose activism and leadership have taught me how to embrace myself, specifically Sonya Renee Taylor, author of *The Body Is Not an Apology*, Taryn Brumfit and the Body Image Movement, and especially, Elizabeth Dialto, Wild Soul Movement maven. Your influence has ripples.

To my Marni, for asking the hard questions and guiding me on the healing path to fully loving myself. Love U!

To my editor, Tanya Gold, for your brilliant and incisive suggestions and for the praise that always arrived just when I needed it most.

To my proofreader, Crystal Watanabe, for your keen eye, careful reading, and kind encouragement.

To my photographers, Cass Bradley and Corrie Fewell, for capturing my power and the beauty of my family in breathtaking photos.

To my fabulous team at SPARK Publications, for understanding my vision, for providing unwavering support, and for helping me share this empowering message with women.

To my Mica, for being my partner, for creating the images that make my words leap off the page. I love them, and I love you.

To my daughters, Campbell Faye and Jude Rae, for being mirrors, for showing me how worthy I am of wide and deep self-love. I hope you always love yourselves and your bodies fiercely, because you are wonderfully made.

To my husband, Terry, who has always loved my body, especially when I couldn't. I love you so, so much. You're my favorite, my touchstone (insert bawdy joke here), my partner in life—thank you for everything.

About the Author

Nicole C. Ayers has been playing with words as long as she can remember. While she's held many jobs in her life, including stints as a server, camp counselor, telemarketer, print-shop lackey, bartender, and teacher, editing at Ayers Edits was her favorite, because she combined her love of reading with the fun of wordplay, until she added writer to this list. Now it would be hard to convince her there's anything better than telling her own stories.

Nicole is the author of *Love Notes to My Body; Love Letters to My Body: Writing My Way to (Self-)Love;* and *Writing Your Way to (Self-)Love: A Guided Journal to Help You Love Your Body, One Part at a Time*.

Nicole lives in South Carolina with her brilliant and brave daughters, her best friend and husband, a goofy dog, a long-suffering tortoise, and the occasional fish.

Connect with Nicole at NicoleCAyers.com and chat with her on Instagram at @nicolecayers.

About the Illustrator

Mica Gadhia was born in Columbus, Ohio, and has lived up and down the East Coast, finally landing in Charlotte, North Carolina, where she lives with her two amazing boys and three lovable cats. Art and bright colors have been a mainstay in her life from the very beginning, and this book was beautifully powerful to work on as her first full-length illustration project.

Mica would love to connect with you at micasworld.com, on Facebook at @micasfunart, and on Instagram at @micasart.

An Invitation

Thank you so much for reading *Love Notes to My Body*. If you're compelled to explore your own relationship with your body, please check out *Writing Your Way to (Self-)Love: A Guided Journal to Help You Love Your Body, One Part at a Time*, where I walk you through my own practice with love and encouragement so that you, too, can give it a whirl.

And if you enjoyed these love notes, you may also enjoy a deeper dive into *Love Letters to My Body: Writing My Way to (Self-)Love*, a collection of personal essays that digs into the grittier side of this journey to accept all the parts of my body. It's vulnerable and honest and poignant.

Please leave a review on Amazon or Goodreads or wherever you purchased the book so that others can find it, too.

Visit my website—NicoleCAyers.com—and sign up for my newsletter, Love Notes, for first looks at new essays, spotlights on people to follow, book recommendations, and more. You can also join me on Instagram at @nicolecayers.

www.ingramcontent.com/pod-product-compliance
Lightning Source LLC
Chambersburg PA
CBHW042111090526
44592CB00005B/84